theory for piano students

by LORA BENNER

**BOOK
ONE**

ED. 2511

G. SCHIRMER, Inc.

DISTRIBUTED BY
HAL•LEONARD®
CORPORATION
7777 W. BLUEMOUND RD. P.O. BOX 13819 MILWAUKEE, WI 53213

FOREWORD

This book provides theoretic knowledge, writing, and playing experience in musical subjects which are related to the first year of piano study. It is also to be used as a first theory text without regard to instrument.

The material is presented in lessons and work sheets to be completed in an eight or nine month term of private or class instruction. The scope of the material may be increased by writing and playing the exercises in additional keys.

The purpose of this book is to supply teachers and pupils with a practical text-work book which combines well organized, comprehensive material with stimulating, instructive presentation to insure good musical development and rapid progress in an interesting way.

L. B.

CONTENTS

Lesson		Page
One	Notes on the Keyboard and Staff	1
	Work Sheet	7
Two	Note Names	9
	Work Sheet	12
Three	Note Values	13
	Work Sheet	16
Four	Time	17
	Work Sheet	20
Five	Half-Steps, Sharps, Flats, Naturals	21
	Work Sheet	25
Six	Rests and Note Values	26
	Work Sheet	28
Seven	Musical Terms, Signs and Whole Steps	29
	Work Sheet	31
Eight	Other Notes and Symbols	32
	Work Sheet	35
Nine	Musical Terms and Intervals	36
	Work Sheet	39
Ten	Music History	40
	Work Sheet	41
Eleven	George Frideric Handel	42
	Work Sheet	43
Twelve	Johann Sebastian Bach	44
	Work Sheet	45
Review Work Sheet		46
Examination		47

Suggested method of study: Two Lessons each month
One month for review
One month for the examination

Lesson One

NOTES ON THE KEYBOARD AND STAFF

KEYBOARD: The White and Black Keys of the piano.

GOING UP the keyboard to the RIGHT ⟶ the tones become *higher* in pitch.

GOING DOWN the keyboard to the LEFT ⟵ the tones become *lower* in pitch.

PITCH: The HIGHNESS or LOWNESS of a tone.

MUSICAL ALPHABET: Seven letters which name the notes.

Going up: A B C D E F G A B C, etc. Say this over and over.

Going down: G F E D C B A G F E, etc. Say this over and over.

BLACK KEY GROUPS and WHITE KEYS on the Piano.

Play all the groups of TWO BLACK KEYS. There are seven of them.

Now, find the TWO BLACK KEY GROUP in the middle of the piano. It is the **fourth** group from the top or from the bottom of the keyboard.

The WHITE KEY just to the left (DOWN) from this two black key group is MIDDLE C.

Every key to the left of each of the two black key groups is called C. There are eight of them on the piano. Play them all.

D is the next white key up from C. It is in the middle of the two black key group. Play all of the Ds.

E is the next white key up from D. It is at the upper end of the two black key group. Play all of the Es.

Now play all the groups of THREE BLACK KEYS. There are seven of them.

Just to the left of each three black key group is F. Play all the Fs.

G is the next white key up from F. It is between the lowest and the middle black keys of the three black key group. Play all the Gs.

A is the next white key up from G. It is between the middle and the highest black key of the three black key group. Play all the As.

B is just to the right of each three black key group. Play all the Bs.

You have now played ALL the WHITE KEYS on the piano.

A MUSICAL STAFF has **FIVE** lines:

A TREBLE CLEF SIGN is usually on the upper staff. Notes on this staff are usually played by the **RIGHT** hand. This clef is sometimes called the **G CLEF**. The **SECOND** line **UP** is G.

Below is a **TREBLE CLEF SIGN**. Draw six more.

A BASS CLEF SIGN is usually on the lower staff. Notes on this staff are usually played by the **LEFT** hand. This clef is sometimes called the **F CLEF**. The **SECOND** line **DOWN** is F.

Below is a **BASS CLEF SIGN**. Draw six more.

A GRAND STAFF has two staffs or staves. They are joined by a vertical line and a brace. Draw more lines and braces.

NOTES are musical figures. They tell HOW LONG a tone is to be held.

When they are ON A STAFF and WITH A CLEF SIGN, they tell *which* tone to play, and *how long* to hold the tone.

NOTES ON THE STAFF

The notes below are both Middle C.

The C nearer the top staff is played by the Right Hand.

The C nearer the lower staff is played by the Left Hand.

EACH LINE and SPACE of the staff holds a different note. You will see this as you play on the piano the notes written on the staffs below. One line or space UP is one note UP on the piano. One line or space DOWN is one note DOWN on the piano.

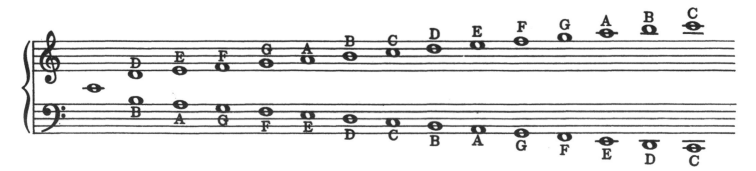

Play the above notes on the piano. Use only one finger.

45446

4

FINGERING - the numbers above or below notes tell which fingers to use to strike the piano keys.

  1 means use the Thumb

  2 means use the Index Finger

  3 means use the Third or Middle Finger

  4 means use the Fourth Finger

  5 means use the Fifth or Little Finger

EAR TRAINING is learning the SOUND of the TONES. This is most important. Play the following notes with your right hand and sing them at the same time: C D E F G. Play the notes again and sing *do re mi fa sol*.

Did you sing the notes in tune with the piano? Now play the following notes with your left hand and sing them at the same time: C B A G F. Play the notes again and sing *do ti la sol fa*.

On the staff below is the SCALE of C Major. It is to be played by the right hand. Play it and sing C D E F G A B C. Then play it again and sing *do re mi fa sol la ti do*.

Now play the Scale of C Major for the left hand and sing C B A G F E D C. Then *do ti la sol fa mi re do*.

There are several ways to remember note names.

Notes in the **SPACES** of the TREBLE CLEF are **F A C E**.

Notes on the **LINES** of the TREBLE CLEF are **E G B D F**. Every Good Boy Does Fine

Notes in the **SPACES** of the BASS CLEF are **A C E G**. All Cows Eat Grass

Notes on the **LINES** of the BASS CLEF are **G B D F A**

Write the names of the notes below each note on the following staves and Remember Them.

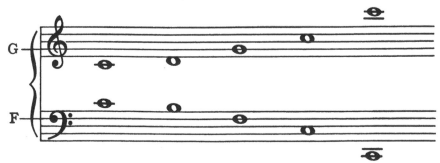

Write the note names below the following notes:

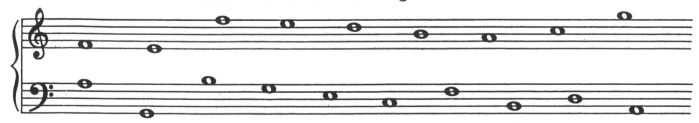

45446

Write the note names below the following notes. Then play what you have written.

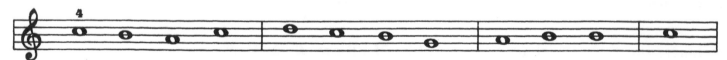

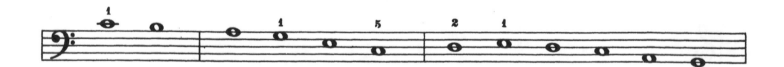

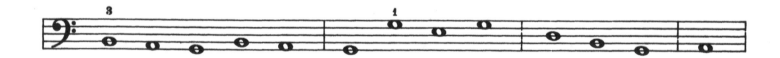

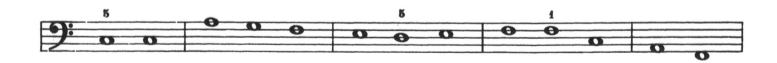

Work Sheet

1   What is the KEYBOARD of a piano? _____

    _____

2   Which direction is UP the keyboard? _____

3   Write the musical alphabet two times going UP. Start with A. _____

    _____

4   Write the musical alphabet two times going DOWN. Start with D. _____

    _____

5   What is another name for TREBLE CLEF? _____

6   What is another name for BASS CLEF? _____

7   On the staffs below:

    a. Draw a bar and brace to make a _____

    b. Draw a CLEF SIGN on each staff.

    c. Draw notes from Middle C to the space above the staff.

    d. Write the note names ABOVE the notes.

    e. Draw notes from Middle C down to the space below staff.

    f. Write the note names BELOW the notes.

8

Write the note names under each note on this sheet.

Write in the fingering where it is not given.

Play and sing what you have written.

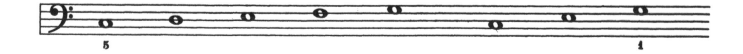

Lesson Two

NOTE NAMES

OCTAVE: an octave is from one note to the next note with the SAME NAME.

The word OCTAVE is used two ways:

1. For TWO NOTES played together which are eight notes apart and have the SAME NAME.

2. For a SERIES of eight notes which begins and ends with notes of the SAME NAME.

On the staff below:

1 Draw in the G Clef sign.

2 Draw notes from Middle C to the A above the staff.

3 Put an × over the two Cs which are an octave apart.

4 Put a ✓ over the two Gs which form an octave.

The MUSICAL ALPHABET by **THIRDS** is every other letter of the musical alphabet.

Going up the alphabet by thirds is A C E G B D F A etc.

Going down the alphabet by thirds is A F D B G E C A etc.

Write this alphabet by thirds going up. Start with F. _____

Write this alphabet by thirds going down. Start with D. _____

A THIRD is from one line to the next line up or down, or one space to the next space up or down on the musical staff.

It skips one note on the piano.

Write the note names under the thirds given below.

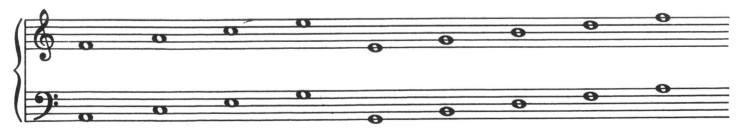

Play these notes.

The MUSICAL ALPHABET by THIRDS is also called the **CHORD ALPHABET.**

Any three notes of it in order form a three-note chord. The name of the note on the bottom is the name of the chord.

Below are notes to play and sing. Write in the missing letter names of the notes for the chords given.

Now play the notes the same way but sing the syllables.

Write the note name under each note given below. Then write the same note an octave higher. Follow the example.

Write the note name above each note given below. Then write the same note an octave lower. Follow the example.

Write the note names over the following notes:

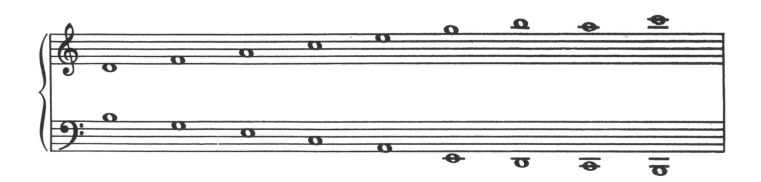

Write notes for the WORDS given. Write *two* notes (octaves) for each letter in both staves. Follow the example given.

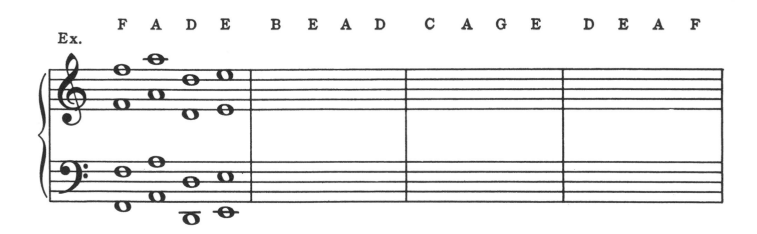

Under each note below, write the note names. Then play what you have written.

Melody for the Right Hand

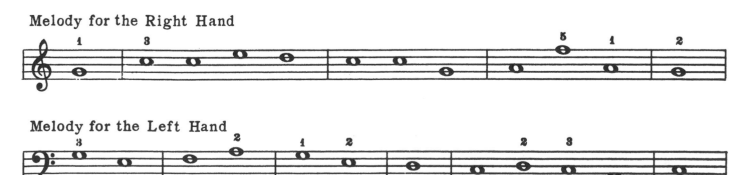

Melody for the Left Hand

Work Sheet

1   What is an OCTAVE? _____

_____

2   In what two ways is the word OCTAVE used? _____

_____

3   Write the Musical Alphabet by Thirds going up. Start with A. _____

_____

4   Write the Musical Alphabet by Thirds going down. Start with E. _____

_____

5   Using whole notes on the staff:
    a. Draw in the TREBLE Clef Sign.
    b. Write the Alphabet by Thirds going up. Start on the notes given.

6   Using whole notes:
    a. Draw in the Bass Clef Sign.
    b. Write the Alphabet by Thirds going up from the first note given.
    c. Write the Alphabet by Thirds going down from the second note given.

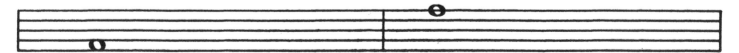

7   What is another name for the alphabet by thirds?

8   On the following staff:
    Write the note names.
    Mark X over the Cs which are octaves apart.
    Mark ✓ over the Es which are an octave apart.
    Mark ○ over the Gs which are an octave apart.

Lesson Three
NOTE VALUES

We have learned that a NOTE is a musical figure which tells HOW LONG a tone is to be held.

Notes have different names for their TIME LENGTHS. We say there are different KINDS of notes.

A **WHOLE NOTE** usually gets **4** beats. ○

A **HALF-NOTE** usually gets **2** beats.

A **QUARTER-NOTE** usually gets **1** beat.

An **EIGHTH-NOTE** usually gets **½** beat.

A **SIXTEENTH-NOTE** usually gets **¼** beat.

A ○ = 2 ♩s   or 4 ♩s   or 8 ♪s   or 16 ♬s

A ♩ = 2 ♩s   or 4 ♪s   or 8 ♬s

A ♩ = 2 ♪s   or 4 ♬s

An ♪ = 2 ♬s

Fill in the following:

A ○ = 4 ____ s;   A ♩ = 2 ____ s;   A ♩ = 2 ____ s.

Fill in the following:

16 ♬s = a ____ ;   8 ♬s = a ____ ;   4 ♩s = a ____ ;   2 ♩s = a ____

8 ♬s = a ____ ;   4 ♪s = a ____ ;   2 ♩s = a ____

4 ♬s = a ____ ;   2 ♪s = a ____

A **DOT** after a note ADDS **½** the time value of the note.

♩• gets 3 beats, 2 beats for the note + 1 beat for the dot.

♩• gets 1½ beats, 1 beat for the note + ½ beat for the dot.

14

UP stems are at the RIGHT (up) side of note heads.

DOWN stems are at the LEFT (down) side of note heads.

Stems go UP when notes are DOWN below the center staff line.

Stems go DOWN when notes are UP above the center staff line.

Stems of notes on the center staff line go the same direction as stems of the nearest notes.

The Stem Length is usually an octave:

Flags are ALWAYS on the RIGHT side of stems.

Eighth-notes and notes of shorter value are often joined in groups by a beam.

Draw stems on the quarter-notes and two half-notes below. Write the note names under the notes and play this melody.

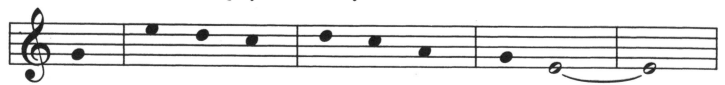

Draw stems and flags or beams if needed on the notes below. Write the note names under the notes and play this melody.

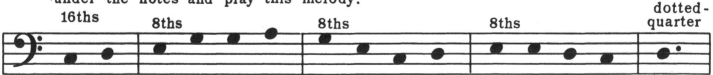

Draw stems, etc. on the following notes. All are quarter-notes except three 8th-notes and one half-note. Write in the Time Signature and note names. Then play it on the piano. Do you know the names of these melodies?

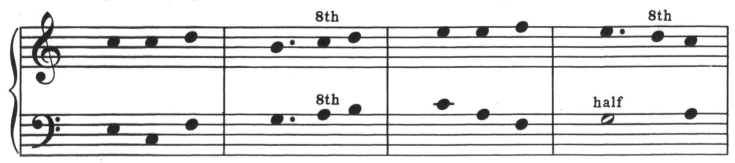

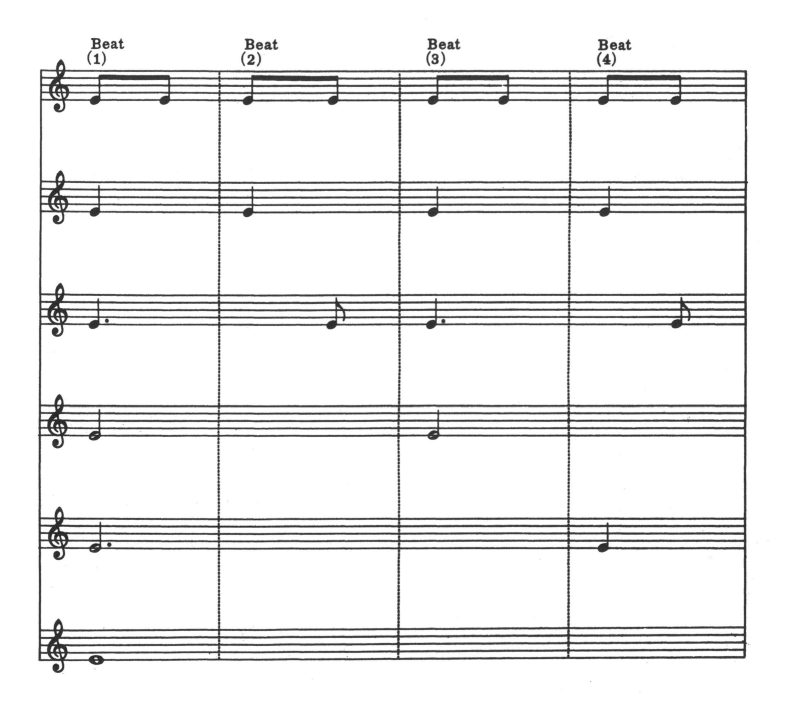

This is a rhythm exercise of one measure – 4 beats. ♩ = 1 beat

Play it with one finger of your right hand and count aloud the numbers 1   2   3   4
    which are the beats of this one measure.

Then play it one octave lower with one finger of your left hand and count the beats aloud.

Work Sheet

1 What two things does a note need to tell which TONE it is? _____

_____

2 What does a note tell WITHOUT these? _____

_____

3 Draw the following:

    a Whole Note _____   a Half-Note, up stem _____

    a Quarter-Note, down stem _____

    an 8th-Note, up stem _____   a 16th-Note, down stem _____

    4—8th-Notes, stems up_____   4—16th-Notes, stems down _____

4 Next to each note or group of notes in question 3, write the number of beats each usually gets.

5 How many beats for a dotted half-note? _____

   How many beats for a dotted quarter? _____

6 How many Half-Notes = a Whole Note? _____

   How many Quarter-Notes = a Whole Note? _____

   How many Eighth-Notes = a Whole Note? _____

7 How many Quarter-Notes = a Half-Note? _____

   How many Eighth-Notes = a Half-Note? _____

8 Put stems on the following notes. Check to see what else is needed and add it.
   Then write note names.

Lesson Four

TIME

At the beginning of every musical composition we find:

1. CLEF SIGNS

2. A KEY SIGNATURE – sharps or flats which tell the key of the piece.

3. A TIME SIGNATURE – two numbers which tell the time of the piece.

   The **TOP** number tells how many beats in each measure.

   The **LOWER** number tells which kind of note gets one beat. This note is sometimes called the beat unit.

$\frac{4}{4}$ time is found most often. This means there are 4 beats in a measure, and a quarter-note gets one beat. This is also called COMMON TIME.

$\frac{3}{4}$ time has 3 beats in a measure, and a quarter-note gets one beat. This is often called WALTZ TIME.

$\frac{2}{4}$ time has 2 beats in a measure, and a quarter-note gets one beat. This is often called MARCH TIME.

$\frac{3}{8}$ and $\frac{6}{8}$ time are also often used. Here an eighth-note gets one beat.

MEASURES are the notes and rests between two Bar-lines. Each MEASURE contains the number of beats given in the top figure of the Time Signature.

Count the beats in the following measures and draw a line through the measure which does NOT have 3 beats (quarter-note gets 1 beat.)

With a **QUARTER-NOTE** as the beat unit, write the number of beats in each measure below.

Number of
beats _____   _____   _____   _____   _____

Add one note to each measure below so that each measure has three beats:

With an 8th-NOTE as the beat unit, write the number of beats in each measure below:

Number of
beats _____   _____   _____   _____   _____

Add one note in each measure so that each measure contains 3 beats with an 8th-note getting 1 beat.

Fill the measures below with 3 beats each - $\frac{3}{4}$ time. Use half-, quarter-, dotted-quarter and 8th-notes.

Play with one finger and count aloud the following rhythm exercise. You can see it is in $\frac{3}{4}$ time.

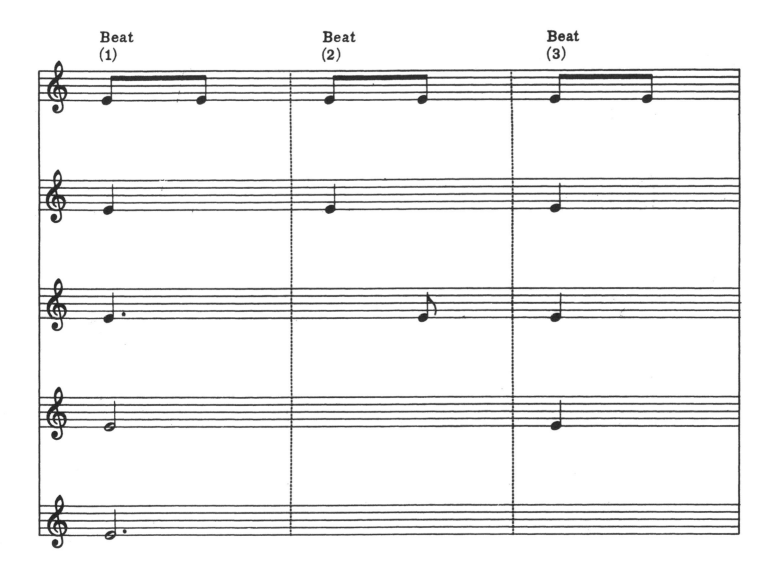

Play and sing the following melody in the correct time with the note names. Then sing it with the syllables. Do you know the name of the song?

Work Sheet

1 Name the three things found at the beginning of a composition.

    a. _____

    b. _____

    c. _____

2 What are **MEASURES?** _____

_____

3 What does each measure contain? _____

_____

4 In a **TIME SIGNATURE,** what does the **TOP** number tell? _____

_____

  What does the **LOWER** number tell? _____

_____

5 What is **COMMON TIME?**   **WALTZ TIME?**   **MARCH TIME?**

6 Tap out the following rhythm on a bench or table.

  If you tap it correctly, you should be able to tell the name of the song without hearing the notes.

Write the name of this song. _____

Lesson Five

HALF-STEPS, SHARPS, FLATS, NATURALS

A **HALF-STEP** is the distance from one tone or piano key to the very next tone. This may be a white key or a black key.

A **SHARP** ♯ raises a tone $\frac{1}{2}$ step.

A **FLAT** ♭ lowers a tone $\frac{1}{2}$ step.

A **NATURAL SIGN** ♮ cancels a sharp or flat.

There are two ways to use sharps, flats, or naturals:

1. In the **KEY SIGNATURE**
2. As **ACCIDENTALS**

KEY SIGNATURES are Sharps or Flats at the beginning of a composition. They are used all through the piece.

ACCIDENTALS are sharps, flats, and natural signs NOT in the key signature but in measures. They apply only to the measure where they are.

SHARPS, FLATS, and **NATURAL SIGNS** are written:

BEFORE the NOTE: ♯♩ ♭♩ ♮♩

AFTER the LETTER: G♯ A♭ B♮

Draw a Sharp: _____ a Flat: _____ a Natural: _____

Draw one sign (sharp, flat, or natural) before each note. Have the middle of the sign on the line or space of its note.

There are 7 WHITE KEYS on the piano called A B C D E F G for notes called A B C D E F G. Each note can be sharped or flatted.

Since there are only 5 BLACK KEYS, we can easily see there must be two White Key sets of sharps and flats.

By looking at the piano, we see these White Key half-steps are between B and C and between E and F.

When we play B♯ we play the key we also call C.
     E♯   F.
     C♭   B.
     F♭   E.

Thus C = B♯   F = E♯   B = C♭   E = F♭

Write this on the staff below - part is given:

BLACK KEYS are also called by two names:
C♯ = D♭,   D♯ = E♭,   F♯ = G♭,   G♯ = A♭,   A♯ = B♭.
    These are **ENHARMONIC NOTES.**

ENHARMONIC – Same tone, Different name

On the staffs below, write notes which are enharmonic to those given. Watch each note carefully!

Write the letter names which are one half-step UP from these given.

C _____ D _____ E _____ or _____ G _____ A _____ B _____ or _____

Write the letter names which are one half-step DOWN from these given.

C _____ or _____ B _____ A _____ G _____ F _____ or _____ E _____ D _____

On the following staves, write notes which are one half-step UP from the notes given.

On the following staves, write notes which are one half-step DOWN from the notes given.

Write the note names above the right hand notes of the top staff.
Write the note names below the left hand notes of the lower staff.

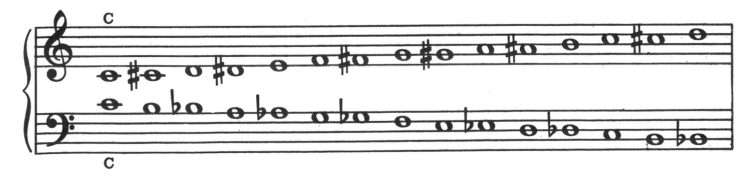

On page 20 we tapped out a rhythm. Did you recognize it? Tap it again.

On the staff below are notes in the same rhythm. Play and sing the tune.

Did you sharp the F? We could have placed the sharp in the key signature because the melody is in the key of G which has one sharp — F sharp.

Below is the same melody in the key of F which has B-flat in the Key Signature. Remember to flat the B when you play it.

Here is the same melody in the Key of C which has no sharps or flats. Sing it in this key. Which key is easiest for you to sing?

Work Sheet

1 Name the two ways sharps or flats are used in a composition.

   a. _____

   b. _____

   Draw a sharp.   What does it do? _____

   _____

   Draw a flat.   What does it do? _____

   _____

   Draw a natural sign.   What does it do? _____

   _____

2 Draw a sharp, flat, or natural sign in the correct place for the following letters and notes:

   G   B   D

3 Name the WHITE KEY SHARPS _____

      WHITE KEY FLATS _____

4 What does ENHARMONIC mean? _____

   _____

5 On the staff below, write the BLACK KEY enharmonic note sets.

6 On the staff below, write the WHITE KEY enharmonic note sets.

Lesson Six

RESTS AND NOTE VALUES

RESTS are very important. Be sure your fingers are not pressing down piano keys when there are rests in the music.

Rests are SILENT beats. They are held for their time length just as notes are held.

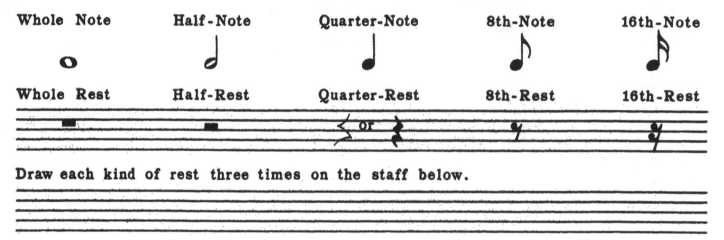

Draw each kind of rest three times on the staff below.

A WHOLE REST is used two ways:

   1 for 4 beats

   2 for a whole measure (no matter how many beats are in the measure.)

TRIPLETS are 3 even notes – same value – which are used to fill the time of 2 of the same kind of notes. A triplet = one beat.

Triplets of quarter-note or longer value notes have ⌐ *3* ⌐ or ⌐ *3* ⌐

Triplets of eighth-notes or shorter value notes are shown

   1 by a ⌢ *3* or ⌣ *3*

   2 by only the figure *3*

   3 by no marking

      Finish the following:

Tap out this rhythm exercise. Be careful to count evenly. Then play it on the piano.

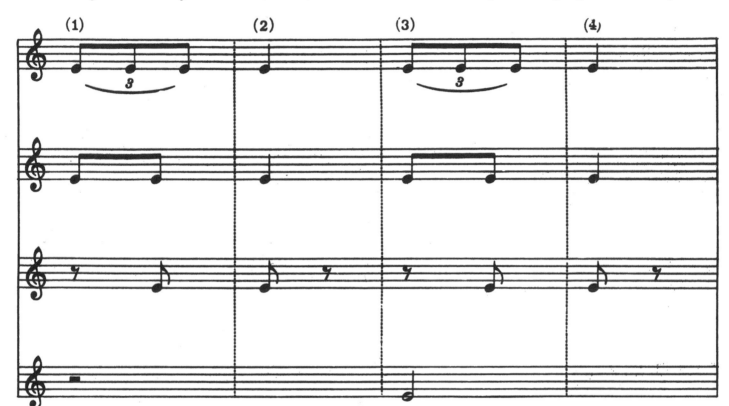

Write in the time signatures. Write note names under the notes of the two melodies given. Then write the syllables under the note names. Sing them both. G is *do* for the Key of G.

G G G D
do do do sol

F is *do* for the Key of F.

F F F C
do do do sol

Work Sheet

1 **Draw rests on the staff below:**

WHOLE	HALF	QUARTER	8th	16th

2 **Complete the following:**

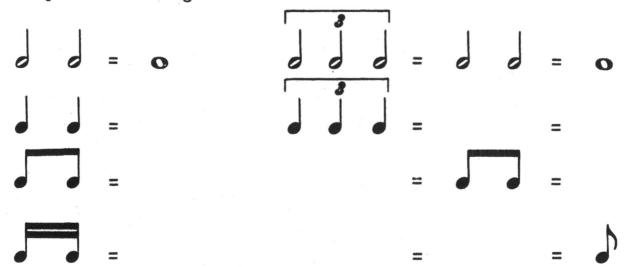

3 **Put in bar-lines for the measures on the following staff.**

  What kind of note gets one beat?

  How many beats in each measure?

4 **Add ONE missing note to each measure below:**

Lesson Seven

MUSICAL TERMS, SIGNS AND WHOLE STEPS

MELODY – One tone after another – or one note at a time. (One person can sing a melody.)

HARMONY – Two or more tones together. (Duets, Trios, Quartets can harmonize.)

RHYTHM – The arrangement of Long and Short Tones.

THEORY – Rule. Theory of Music. = Rules of Music.

ACCENT – Stress. Play an accented note louder.

MEASURE ACCENT – Stress on the first note in a measure.

LEGATO – Smooth (Each tone joins the next tone.)

STACCATO – Short (Each tone is separated.)

SLUR ⌒ a curved line over or under notes ♩♩♩ (They are to be played *legato* with the last note a bit shorter in time.)

TIE ⌒ a curved line from one note to the very next note which is the same tone. ♩♩ Play the first note ONLY – but hold through time value of both notes.

♩ ♪ = ♩. Hold 1½ beats (if a quarter-note gets 1 beat.)

♩ ♩ = ♩. Hold 3 beats (if a quarter-note gets 1 beat.)

Count the beats in each measure below. A ♩ gets 1 beat.

Write in the TIME SIGNATURE. Notice the first and last notes equal one whole measure.

45446

Play the following melody. Be sure to play the first note of each measure a little louder than the other notes — but not longer.

Below is a melody to tap. You should know the name of it if your rhythm is right. Write in TIME SIGNATURE. ♩ = 1 beat.

A **WHOLE STEP** is TWO HALF-STEPS. Since there are only 2 sets of white key half-steps on the piano the others are white key **WHOLE STEPS**.

Play these whole steps on the piano — C–D, D–E, F–G, G–A, A–B

Also play these whole steps E – F#, B – C#, F – E♭, C – B♭

On the staff below, write notes one WHOLE STEP up from those given.

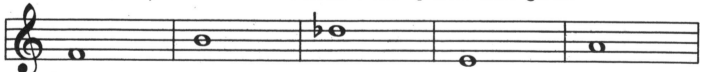

On the staff below, write notes one whole step down from those given.

Work Sheet

1 What is MELODY? _____

2 What is HARMONY? _____

3 What is RHYTHM? _____

4 How do you play LEGATO? _____

5 How do you play STACCATO? _____

6 What is an ACCENT? _____

7 How do you play notes that are under a slur?_____

8 Write two notes tied which = the dotted notes below.

       𝅝• =   ♩. =

       𝅗𝅥• =   ♪. =

9 On the staff below, write notes one WHOLE step up from those given.

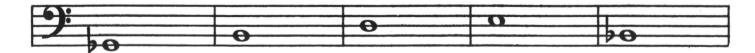

10 On the staff below, write notes one WHOLE step down from those given.

Lesson Eight

OTHER NOTES AND SYMBOLS

When notes are to be played together, they are on the same side of the same stem UNLESS they are on a line and the next space. (There would not be room for each note on the same side in this case.)

NOTES ABOVE and BELOW the STAFF

Notice that:

2 Lines *above* the staff is 2 octaves above Middle C.

2 Lines *below* the staff is 2 octaves below Middle C.

NOTES BETWEEN the STAFFS

How notes are written between staffs show which hand plays them. Play this on the piano.

DOUBLE BARS are at the end of a composition or at the end of a definite section of it.

REPEAT SIGNS mean play the music two times – either from the beginning of the piece to the Repeat sign (see Ex.1) or the music enclosed by the signs (see Ex.2).

Ex.1   Ex.2

FIRST and **SECOND ENDINGS** are used when the end of the part to be repeated is different. Play through the First Ending, repeat up to it, skip it, and play the Second Ending. Play each ending just *once*.

D.C. means Da Capo – from the beginning

    Go back to the beginning and play.

D.S. means Dal Segno – from the sign 𝄋

    Go back to the sign and play

FINE means end.

    D.C. al Fine – go back to beginning and play to Fine.

    D.S. al Fine – go back to 𝄋 and play to Fine.

CODA – a few measures added to the end of a composition to make a fancier finish. The word means tail.

PHRASING – the grouping of notes into rhythmic sections. These notes are often under a slur. Good phrasing is MOST IMPORTANT.

Below are syllables for the notes in three keys

	1–DO	2–RE	3–MI	4–FA	5–SOL	6–LA	7–TI	8–DO
Key of C	C	D	E	F	G	A	B	C
Key of G	G	A	B	C	D	E	F♯	G
Key of F	F	G	A	B♭	C	D	E	F

In Lesson 7 you tapped out the rhythm of a melody. Did you call it *London Bridge?* Here are the syllables in the key of C. Play and sing it.

Write the same melody on the following staff in the key of G. Write in the syllables. Play and sing it.

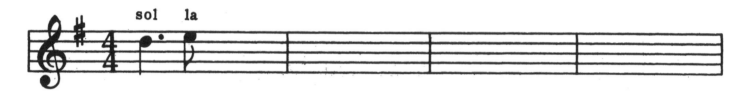

Write in the key signature and time signature for the same melody in the key of F on the staff below. Then write in the notes and syllables. Play and sing it.

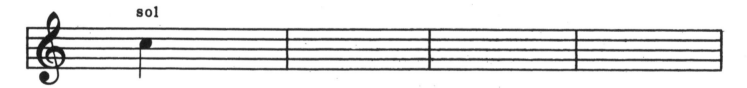

Or did you hear *Mary Had a Little Lamb?* Here it is in the key of G. It has the same melodic rhythm as *London Bridge*.

Can you write *Mary Had a Little Lamb* in the key of C?

Work Sheet

1 On the staffs below:

    a. Draw the treble clef and bass clef signs.

    b. Write the names of the notes given.

    c. In measures 1 and 3 write notes an octave below the notes given.

    d. In measures 2 and 4 write notes an octave above the notes given.

2 What does each of the following mean?

    a. D.C. _____

    b. D.S. _____

    c. Fine _____

    d. D.C. al Fine _____

3 If a piece has a 1st and 2nd ending, how many times do you play each ending? ____

_____

4 What is PHRASING? _____

_____

5 Complete the following:

Key Signature	Note Name	Syllable
G		Sol
F	B♭	

Lesson Nine
MUSICAL TERMS AND INTERVALS

Most musical terms are Italian. This is because much of the early music was Church music, and Rome was the center of this activity.

f   *Forte* Loud

ff *Fortissimo* Very Loud

p   *Piano* Soft

pp *Pianissimo* Very Soft

Una Corde use Soft Pedal

m   *Mezzo* (pronounced metso) medium

mf *Mezzo Forte* Medium Loud

mp *Mezzo Piano* Medium Soft

Crescendo-(Cresc.) Gradually Louder

Decrescendo-(Decresc.) Gradually Softer

Swell   Gradually Louder, then softer

Rit.   *Ritardando* gradually slower

Rall. *Rallentando* gradually slower

Accel. *Accelerando* gradually faster

Allegro   fast, lively tempo

Andante moderate tempo

Adagio   very slow tempo

Tempo overall speed (of the music or rhythm)

A Tempo return to the original tempo (speed) after playing faster or more slowly.

Fermata   a pause, a hold

8va or *8* - - - - - - - means play one octave higher than written

8va bassa or *8* - - - - - - - play one octave lower than written

\>   Accent placed over or under note to be stressed.

—   Accent placed over or under note to be stressed.

Damper Pedal — pedal on right. It raises the dampers from the strings and allows them to vibrate freely.

An **INTERVAL** is the difference in pitch between two tones. We say, an interval is the difference between any two notes.

The difference between the two notes is the SIZE of the Interval. Measure the size by counting the lines and spaces from the bottom to the top note. Include the lines or spaces which hold both notes.

On the staff below are intervals and their size. Count each one so that you understand how to do this.

On the following staff, write notes above those given to make the sized interval written under the notes.

There are two ways to write or play an interval:

MELODIC INTERVAL $\left(\begin{array}{l}\text{one tone or}\\\text{note at a time}\end{array}\right)$ **HARMONIC INTERVAL** $\left(\begin{array}{l}\text{played}\\\text{together}\end{array}\right)$

You can see that you have been playing melodic intervals from your first lesson.

On the staff below, write the size under each interval and write M if it is Melodic or H if it is Harmonic.

On the staff below: First play Middle C and sing it. Then sing each interval BEFORE
you play it. Can you do this?

Tap the following rhythm with the expression given:

Play the notes below with the same rhythm and expression.

On the staff below, finish drawing slurs under the phrases. Notice that these phrases
form similar musical patterns.

See if you can finish the phrases in each measure. Study the first phrase pattern to
help you fill in the missing notes.

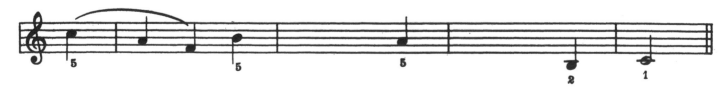

Now play these two melodies. Use the fingering given.

Work Sheet

1   Write the letters used for the following terms and the meaning of each:

fortissimo _____

forte _____

pianissimo _____

piano _____

mezzo _____

2   Draw symbols for the following:

    a. *crescendo*

    b. *decrescendo*

    c. *swell*

3   How do you play when you see *rit.* _____

                              accel. _____

4   What do the following terms mean?

allegro _____

adagio _____

andante _____

5   Under the staff below, write the size of the intervals and M for Melodic or
      H for Harmonic.

6   On the staff below, draw the intervals named.

    M3   H4   H6   M7   H5

Lesson Ten

MUSIC HISTORY

Not much is known about the very beginning of music. Most musicians feel it probably began with rhythm in a very simple form.

Next probably came song as men grunted or cried in various pitches.

The beginning of our music, so far as we know, was five hundred and forty years after the birth of Christ (540 A.D.). CHANTS, which are very simple melodies with very little change of pitch, were used then. Pope Gregory selected chants to teach other church men.

In 1,000 A.D. a monk named Guido, who was also a teacher, put notes on lines. He fixed the intervals of whole and half-steps. Guido had a staff with four lines. The fifth line was added later. He also named the notes: *ut, re, mi, fa, sol, la. Ut* was later changed to *do* and *ti* was added.

There were two main keyboard instruments in use before the piano. One was a Clavichord; the other was a Harpsichord. The Piano was invented around 1711 by an Italian named Cristofori. He built his piano to order for the Medici family. It was called a Pianoforte (soft-loud) because it was the first keyboard instrument which could play both soft and loud.

Bach and Handel played both the Harpsichord and Clavichord. Bach played and wrote music for both. Handel preferred the Harpsichord.

These two great composers were twenty-six years old before the piano was invented. They were both famous on their instruments which were perfect at that time. While both saw and played pianos, they did not like those early ones which were not like the pianos we have today.

However, the music of both these great composers can be played on the piano even though it was written for other instruments.

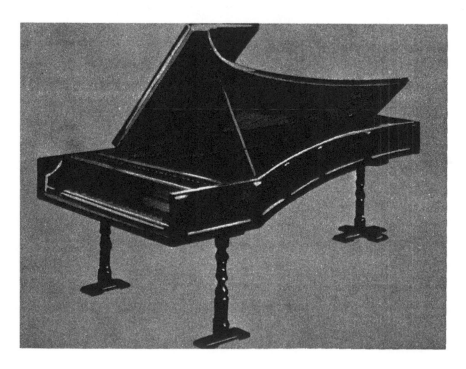

Cristofori Pianoforte

Work Sheet

1   Draw a line under which probably came first and a circle around which probably came second.

Melody   Harmony   Rhythm

2   Who put notes on lines and spaces and named them? _____

_____

3   What two keyboard instruments were used before the piano? _____

_____

_____

4   Who invented the piano? _____

5   What was it then called? _____

6   On the staff below, write the same notes but for the RIGHT HAND to play that are given here for the LEFT HAND to play.

7   On the staff below:

     a. Draw a Treble Clef Sign.

     b. Put in the bar-lines.

     c. Play on the piano.

     d. Put accidentals where they belong.

     e. In what Key is it? _____

Lesson Eleven

GEORGE FRIDERIC HANDEL (1685-1759)

Handel was born February 24, 1685, twenty-five days before Bach. He was born at Halle, Germany. His father was a barber-surgeon who earned a living doing both. There were no musicians in the family before George.

By the time he was twelve years old, Handel played the organ, harpsichord, violin, oboe and other instruments. He had composed pieces before he was ten years old and was famous by the time he was fifteen.

When he was eighteen years old he went to Lübeck, Germany to try to get a position as organist there. He could have had the position, but he found he would have to marry the old organist's daughter. Two years later Bach turned down the same position for the same reason.

Handel lived in Italy for four years. The operas he wrote there were successful. He was well known in many countries. He moved to London when he was twenty-five.

Handel was a fine musician and played and composed music for many instruments, but he was noted at first mainly for his operas. He not only wrote them, he staged them and sold tickets for their performances. He made quite a bit of money in this way.

When people became tired of operas, he lost his money and was very poor. Then he began to write oratorios. These are dramatic musical compositions based on stories of the Bible. He also staged some of these and once again made a great deal of money. His most famous oratorio is the *Messiah* which is sung all over the world many times every year.

Handel was a kind and thoughtful man. He loved children and helped to start the Foundling Home for orphaned children in London. Every year he gave a concert to raise money for the Home.

Handel probably never heard of Bach, but Bach had certainly heard of Handel. Once Bach walked twenty-five miles to Halle to meet Handel. Handel did not know Bach was coming and had left for London.

Handel never married. When he was sixty-six years old, he became ill and blind. The surgeon who operated on his eyes also was Bach's doctor. Handel lived to be seventy-four which was quite old in those days.

Work Sheet

1 In what year was Handel born? _____

2 What other musician was born the same year? _____

3 What instrument of the piano family did Handel play? _____

_____

4 What did his father do for a living? _____

_____

5 In what country did Handel write operas before going to London? _____

_____

6 What is the name of his most famous oratorio? _____

_____

7 Tap out the rhythm of the following Christmas songs and name them.

Name _____

Name _____

8 On the staff below, complete the WHITE key enharmonic sets. Write the note names under each note.

B♯ =   B =

Lesson Twelve

JOHANN SEBASTIAN BACH (1685-1750)

Unlike Handel, Bach came from a very musical family. His father was a court musician and taught Bach to play the violin and viola. He died when Bach was only nine years old.

Then Johann went to live with an older brother who also earned his living as a musician. His brother taught Bach to play the organ and the clavichord.

From the time he was fifteen, Bach held many church positions and became noted for his wonderful organ playing. He also wrote a great deal of music.

Although he was never wealthy, Bach always earned a good living. He was a fine husband and father. When his first wife died, Bach married another good woman named Anna Magdalena. She was also a musician. Bach had twenty children! Three of his sons became famous musicians. Bach wrote many pieces for his wife, his children and other pupils.

When he was thirty-eight years old, Bach became head of St. Thomas school at Leipzig. He spent the rest of his life there except for short trips around Germany to test and to play organs. He never left Germany during his life and was not known elsewhere.

Bach taught many subjects at the school. He also had many private pupils and conducted orchestras, choruses and choirs. He wrote a song a week for the choirs—over 265 songs! He also composed masses which are large religious works. He wrote music for the organ, the clavier, violin and other instruments. He even engraved his own music! No one can understand how he could do so much. And everything was perfect.

With all this writing and engraving, it is no wonder his eyesight gave out. After he died, his music was handed down from one great musician to another, but few others knew of him for over 75 years after his death. Then Felix Mendelssohn performed Bach's *St. Matthew Passion* in public. A society was formed just to find and to publish Bach's music.

Many musicians think he was the greatest genius of all. Certainly everyone who plays the piano should study and play pieces by Bach.

Work Sheet

1 In what year was Bach born? _____

2 How many children did he have? _____

3 How many of them became famous musicians? _____

4 Did Bach ever leave Germany? _____

5 What happened to both Bach and Handel? _____

_____

6 Did Bach come from a musical family? _____

7 Did Handel come from a musical family? _____

8 On the staff below, write the BLACK key enharmonic note sets.

C♯ =

9 Write the note names and syllables for the following:

10 When sharps or flats are at the beginning of a composition and the beginning of each line, what are they called?

_____

11 When sharps or flats are found in certain measures of a composition, what are they called? _____

_____

12 What is Common Time? _____ Waltz Time? _____ March Time? _____

Review Work Sheet

Write two notes on each staff for every letter given:

C A B   B E D   F E D   G A D

Write the number of beats for each measure in the following time signatures:

$\frac{2}{4}$ ____ $\frac{3}{4}$ ____ $\frac{4}{4}$ ____ $\frac{6}{8}$ ____ $\frac{9}{16}$ ____ $\frac{12}{16}$ ____ $\mathbf{C}$ ____

Draw the note which gets one beat after each of the following time signatures:

$\frac{2}{4}$ $\frac{6}{8}$ $\frac{9}{16}$ $\frac{3}{2}$ $\mathbf{C}$

Complete the following:

𝅝 = 2   s,   4   s,   8   s,   16   s

𝅗𝅥 = 2   s,   4   s,   8   s

♩ = 2   s,   4   s

♪ = 2   s

𝅗𝅥. = 3   s

♩. = 3   s

Examination

I   On the ledger lines below:

1   Make a Grand Staff.

2   Draw the Clef Signs.

3   Write a Time Signature showing three beats in a measure with a quarter-note the beat unit.

4   Write the note names above or below the notes.

5   Draw stems on the notes.

6   Draw bar-lines where they belong.

7   Draw double bars where they belong.

8   On the upper staff, write a dotted half-note an octave below the last note.

9   On the lower staff, write a dotted half-note an octave below the last note.

10 What is another name for this time signature? _____

II   What is another name for:

1   Treble Clef? _____

2   Bass Clef? _____

III Write the musical alphabet by thirds:

    1 Going up, start with E. _____

    2 Going down, start with E. _____

    3 What is the other name for this alphabet? _____

    _____

IV What is a note? _____

    1 What does it tell without a staff? _____

    _____

    2 What does it tell with a staff and clef sign? _____

    _____

V Name and draw four kinds of notes.

    Write the number of usual beats after each note above.

    What does a dot after a note add? _____

    _____

    What does a dot above or below a note mean? _____

    _____

    Draw a triplet of 8th-notes.

    How do you count this? _____

VI What are the two uses of a whole rest?

      1 _____

      2 _____

On the top staff, write a note of a different time value in each measure.

On the lower staff, write a rest with the same time value as the note above it.

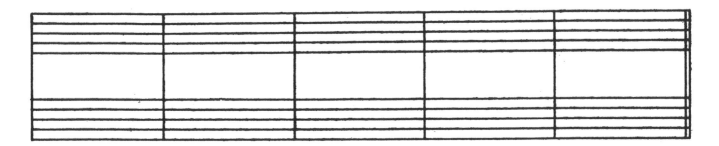

VII If a ♩ gets one beat, write the number of beats in each of the following measures:

Add ONE missing note to each measure below:

Add TWO missing notes to each measure below:

Add THREE notes to each measure below:

Fill in the two blanks:

If a ♩ gets 1 beat, a ♩. = _____ beats, a ○. = _____

VIII Draw a sharp   a flat   a natural sign

Draw one of these for each of the following:

C   G   F   O   O   O

What is an accidental? _____

_____

How is it used? _____

What are Enharmonic tones? _____

_____

On the staff below, draw four sets of enharmonic tones.

IX   When 1st and 2nd endings are used, how many times is each ending played? _____

What is Phrasing? _____

_____

What do the following mean?

legato _____

staccato _____

accent _____

measure accent _____

allegro _____

andante _____

adagio _____

X   On the staff below, write notes which are one WHOLE step UP from the notes given:

Write notes which are one HALF-step DOWN from the notes given:

Write intervals of the size and type given below.

On the staff below, write the note names and syllable names under the notes in the spaces given. Add slurs for the similar patterns.

Name _____

Syllable _____

On the staff below, write the same melody in the Key of F.